JAMIE MORRISON, PA-C

EMBRACE
THE
SHADOW

Within

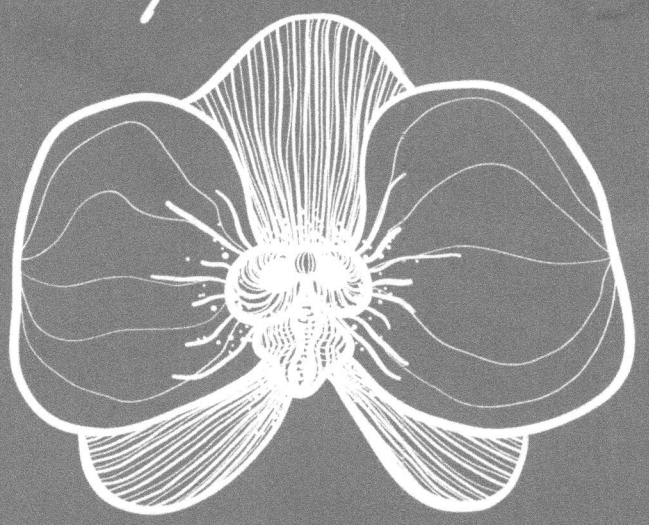

THE 30 DAY SHADOW WORK GUIDE
WITH LETTERS FROM THE WISE.

Introduction

The initial purpose of this work was to guide women towards a journey of self-discovery. However, while writing, I realized this journey is a constant evolution that applies to everyone, irrespective of gender.

As someone raised in the Baptist faith, I was familiar with biblical verses but still had unanswered questions. This internal conflict inspired me to embark on a spiritual journey. I questioned my beliefs and explored various religious practices, including Theism, Atheism, and African Traditional Religions. What I discovered was that each path led to a higher power, a source of all-encompassing knowledge and understanding. Despite having different names and views about this source, it unites us all. This realization was a profound epiphany, shaped by perception.

Perception is the lens through which we experience life, influencing our every decision. Some perceptions are innate; others are taught. What if we are all connected, regardless of our physical differences or spiritual beliefs? For instance, plants release oxygen, which we breathe in, while we exhale carbon dioxide, which plants absorb. It's a symbiotic relationship. Could everything happening around us also be a symbiotic relationship, a manifestation of the Yin and Yang concept?

From a young age, we are indoctrinated with the gender roles and societal expectations that shape our lives. We're encouraged to pursue Prince Charming or Mrs. Right, acquire wealth, complete college education, settle down, and start a family. We rarely consider the idea of seeking happiness and fulfillment within ourselves first.

I encourage embarking on a journey of self-discovery, free from prejudices or expectations. It's my strong belief happiness, growth, and spiritual balance stem from within. I, too, made the mistake of seeking love outside of myself, which resulted in a constant cycle of unhappiness, depression, self-hate, and low self-esteem.

Unfortunately, it took 38 years of life to finally accept and love myself as I am, but that's what has fueled my journey to self-love. When you learn to love yourself, you gain the power to shape your path in life, manifest your dreams, and teach others how you deserve to be treated. Your worth should never be solely dependent on someone else's opinion of you; perception is not a fact. Take control of your worth – that's how you learn to be truly happy in this world.

I hope this journal serves as a guide to help you understand that genuine happiness can only be achieved by you. It's something you must learn to attain on your journey through life. It's meant to offer guidance from The Wise, something I didn't have when I needed it.

As women, we have the power to uplift one another and help our younger generations grow into strong, worthy, and empowered individuals. The truth is, the wise woman we seek is within us every step of the way.

Our experiences, both successful and challenging, contribute to our wisdom. Our journey is not a source of shame but rather an opportunity to learn invaluable lessons. It's time to manifest the wise woman within you, one who possesses self-love, self-worth, and self-acceptance. To accomplish this, the wise woman needs a voice, which can only be achieved through self-knowledge.

I strive daily to empower the wise woman within me, which eventually replaces the fearful, self-loathing woman. Growing into a wise woman is possible for each of us, as maturity is not necessarily a function of age. I share my journey with the hope others will join me in becoming a mature woman who can help guide the next generation. Now is the time to delve deep and begin the journey of shadow work.

With Love,
Jamie

GLIMPSE WITHIN YOUR SOUL'S
WINDOW TO EMBRACE YOUR

Shadow

RULES
OF
Engagement

OUR HIGHER SELF IS WHO WE ARE AT THE CORE, A FRAGMENT OF THE SOURCE THAT IS A PART OF ALL OF US, NO MATTER THE AGE, SITUATION, OR TIME. IT IS THE ESSENCE WE REVERT TO, AND WE ARE ALL FRAGMENTED BUT CONNECTED.

Soul

Feeling Scale

Shadow work can be a challenging process, as it involves confronting and processing difficult emotions we may have initially suppressed. To aid in this process, I've developed a feeling scale. By becoming more attuned to our emotional states, we can better navigate through our shadow side.

Assess your emotional state using the Feeling Scale both before and after performing shadow work. Additionally, it's crucial to have a self-care activity planned that you can engage in following the shadow work activity.

Rules of Engagement

Shadow work is not about validating right or wrong. Rather, it's about acknowledging and comprehending the journey. Each of us is akin to a unique, rare, and precious stone. Such precious crystals and stones are formed over time through years of intense pressure and hard work.

1. Be patient with yourself

Yes, this is a 30 day guide but shadow work is for you and there is no rushing internal healing.

2. No negative self talk

Imagine yourself as an innocent child. Would you ever talk down to that child or say things to intentionally inflict emotional pain? If not, then why subject yourself to such behavior? If you would, it's vital to address the underlying issues causing such behavior. No child should ever experience emotional trauma due to an adult's unaddressed wounds.

3. Don't make it personal

During this process, some memories, anger, or pain may resurface. However, it is essential to remember that the healing is primarily for you. It's not about seeking validation, although that may be a byproduct. It's about embracing the journey you've walked, including the challenges you've faced. It's crucial to acknowledge not everything that happened was a direct result of your actions. Thus, it's important to allow yourself to focus on your healing and forgiveness, rather than the person, place, or thing that may have caused the pain.

Never hesitate to identify when certain topics are too tough for you to navigate alone. Always seek help whether it be family, friends, emergency response, safe circles, or therapy. We all go through changes. There is beauty in each season of our lives!

4. No lashing out

This might be a challenging task that can occasionally lead to overwhelming emotions and frustrations. Nevertheless, understanding your shadow self is crucial to relinquish any spiritual or emotional burdens that might be obstructing you from achieving your life's goals. Reacting impulsively will only hinder the progress and add further scars. Instead, it's essential to focus on attaining self-control. If you're reading this, it's likely you've endured enough pain. Hence, it's time to embrace a different approach.

What if I can't adhere to the rules of engagement?

Shadow work is a spiritual exploration that delves beyond the physical realm. It's vital to be spiritually prepared before embarking on this journey. In the event you haven't reached that point yet, it's advisable to redirect your focus towards meditation, fostering inner peace, and improving self-control.
Your Spirit is well aware of the most opportune time and setting for you to embark on your spiritual healing expedition. Please refer to the self-care section and devote a minimum of thirty minutes every day to purify your energy and promote inner peace.

PAIN IS A TEMPORARY FEELING
NEEDED TO BREAK THE OUTER SHELL
OF

Understanding

SELF CARE

Ideas

YOUR ENDING DOES NOT HAVE TO
LOOK LIKE YOUR

Beginning

Herbal Tea

Numerous herbs possess medicinal properties and have been utilized for centuries to treat various health conditions. It's noteworthy that store-bought herbs tend to be less potent than fresh-grown. Therefore, it's essential to exercise caution when making your selection.

Herb	Property
Chamomile	Relaxing
Lavender	Antidepressant
Ginger	Digestive tonic
Dandelion	Diuretic
Tumeric	Anti-inflammatory
Lemon	Detoxifying
Tea	Stimulant
Black Cohosh	Hormonal Tonic

While herbal medicine can be beneficial, it's not FDA approved and should not be used as a substitute for prescribed medication. It's crucial to consult with your Primary Care Provider when dealing with any medical conditions.

Meditation

Meditation takes practice, but I highly recommend this practice. Start with 3–5 minutes and increase over time. Create a place in your mind you go to for mediation. You can meditate to the sound of nature, meditation music, or Tibetan bowls. Let this place be your mental vacation space. Meditation helps to relax your mind and provides a peaceful escape for spiritual focus.

As you continue to practice meditation, you'll notice an improvement in your overall well-being. Regular meditation can help to reduce stress, anxiety, and depression. It also promotes emotional health, improves concentration and memory, and enhances self-awareness.

One of the most significant benefits of meditation is its ability to help you connect with your spirituality. Whether you follow a specific religion or not, meditation can help you feel more connected to yourself, others, and the world around you.

If you're new to meditation, there are many resources available to help you get started. Books, online videos, and guided meditation apps can all be helpful tools as you begin your practice. The key to successful meditation is consistency and patience. With time and practice, you'll find that meditation becomes an essential part of your daily routine, providing a sense of calm and inner peace that will benefit you for years to come.

Prayer & Mantra

Incorporating daily mantras into your routine is a highly rewarding practice. Whether you choose to focus on love, gratitude, peace, or strength, affirmations can help you realign your focus and raise your vibrations. Prayer is another powerful tool that can aid in establishing a deep and personal connection with the Creator. Communication is key to building this relationship, so don't hesitate to foster it through prayer or simple conversation. Regardless of the path you take to connect with the Creator, prayer and mantras remain valuable tools. Customize your practice to create a space that feels right for you – light candles, create a prayer closet or room, build an altar, or venture to a peaceful outdoor location. Trust that your spirit will guide you to what is best for you.

Spiritual Bath

A spiritual bath is not only a means to relax your muscles but also to cleanse your soul. This bath isn't intended for physical cleaning, so it's crucial to have a shower or bath beforehand to ensure your body is clean, serving as a pure vessel for the spiritual bath.

There are various ways to enjoy a spiritual bath, including incorporating different types of salts such as Dead Sea salt, Pink Himalayan salt, or Epsom salt. Candles set a relaxing open atmosphere. You can also add essential oils to your bath to achieve specific purposes, such as peace, love, protection, or manifestation.

Moreover, herbs are another crucial ingredient that can be used in your bath. You can grind them to reduce clogging or place them in a tea or muslin bag. Alternatively, you can choose to let the herbs free float in your bath to appreciate their beauty.

Whenever you are feeling troubled or unsettled spiritually, consider turning to a spiritual bath to achieve relaxation and clarity of mind.

SELF

Assessment

Self-Assessment

What wound, trauma, or heartbreak are you carrying?

What were the things about the act that caused you pain?

Can you say that you were valued by looking at how you were treated? Explain why or why not.

What action did you take to value and protect yourself in the situation?

What were your expectations in the situation?

Were these expectations realistic when you think back on the character of this person or actions leading up to the event?

Did you make excuses to accept their behavior and avoid the red flags?

Self-Assessment

After heartbreak have you ever chosen to be a "Playerette" or "Independent Woman?" How did you handle the hurt?

While employing either of these methods did you ever feel lonely? List examples of those lonely moment.

Did the relationships that caused you to adopt this thought process start with an individual who was initially worthy of you? Or did you lower yourself, and if so, why?

Do you feel that choosing the "Playerette" or "Independent woman" life solved loneliness? What was the outcome? Did it bring love into your life or more heartbreak?

Self-Assessment

It's not uncommon to experience heartbreak so profound it manifests as physical pain. Have you encountered such a situation?

If so, what measures did you adopt to alleviate or cope with the agony?

Did your approach help you overcome the pain? Was it a temporary or permanent solution?

Were there any obstacles that impeded your healing process?

Have you taken steps to prioritize or eliminate these obstacles?

Now that you've identified these obstructions, what's holding you back from addressing them?

Self-Assessment

Have you given access to your spiritual gateway to others? Consider the following:

- Were they deserving of your trust? Think about their actions and motivations.

- Were they worth the health of your body or spirit?

- What qualities are necessary for someone to even be considered for access to your spiritual gateway?

Moving forward, it's crucial not to sacrifice these requirements. To your future self, remember that patience and discernment are key to maintaining the integrity of your spiritual journey.

Commit to self

Create 5 promises that you can refer back to when you feel yourself falling back into the same situations or relationships habits that normally leave you with heartbreak. Refer to them whenever you are feeling weak.

1.

2.

3.

4.

5.

Forgiveness is for you! Remember shadow work is not about placing blame but gaining understanding.

YOUR
JOURNEY
Begins

YOUR TRUE SELF LIES

Within

Cleanse

During week 1 of your journey, your primary objective is to identify any emotional trauma and triggers you may be carrying and work towards freeing yourself from them. While this process can be taxing and may involve confronting difficult memories, remember you're not alone. Many individuals undergo a similar process while embarking on a journey of self-exploration.

A helpful method is to begin by examining your past experiences and identifying negative patterns or recurring themes. Once you have a better understanding of these patterns, it's possible to delve into the root causes of such traumas and triggers. This may necessitate working with a therapist or counselor or taking time to reflect and journal your thoughts and feelings.

As you address and process these emotions, you may encounter a range of feelings, including sadness, anger, relief, and joy. It's important to be kind and patient with yourself during this phase and to take breaks as necessary.

Ultimately, this cleansing process aims to let go of past traumas and move forward with greater clarity and purpose. By releasing these blockages and traumas, you create room for new growth and opportunities in your life.

Week 1

Connect with Nature

THE ESSENCE OF LIFE IS PRESENT WITHIN ALL LIVING BEINGS. HOWEVER, THE CHAOS OF THE WORLD, AS PERCEIVED THROUGH OUR LIMITED PERSPECTIVE, CAN OBSCURE THE SOOTHING ENERGY OF THE EARTH. OUR CONNECTION WITH THIS VIBRANT, LIVING CREATION IS SYMBIOTIC BUT WE OFTEN DISREGARD IT DUE TO OUR LACK OF SPIRITUAL AWARENESS. TAKING TIME TO CONNECT WITH NATURE CAN ELEVATE OUR VIBRATIONS, PROVIDING ANSWERS TO THE QUESTIONS THAT WEIGH US DOWN.

Letter from The Wise

He was just as handsome as I had imagined, yet I couldn't ignore the nagging feeling he was trouble. It was evident from the moment he tapped my thigh upon our initial introduction, which in hindsight was a disrespectful gesture towards a stranger, especially a woman.

His penetrating gaze and ardent pursuit of me were overwhelming, and I found myself succumbing to his charm. But once we slept together, his demeanor grew distant, almost frosty, and he seemed content with a more platonic relationship.

It became apparent he was only interested in my talents and success in areas he was passionate about, as well as my body. He wanted to have his cake and eat it too, and I struggled with mixed signals and confusion about his intentions.

Eventually, I realized he lacked empathy and was solely focused on his happiness, regardless of how his actions affected others, including myself. It dawned on me that I was being used, and while I was initially angry, I later realized that it was not entirely his fault; he was responsible for his own life and choices. However, his actions were undoubtedly wrong and harmful.

I realized the disappointment I felt was a result of not heeding my intuition. From the very beginning, I knew my interactions with this person would not end well. Despite warning him about this, I failed to listen to my inner voice. A tiny voice within me cautioned me every time I was in his presence, but I was swayed by his charming looks and physique. I lacked the strength to keep our relationship platonic as he always seemed to be exploiting me both mentally and sexually, and I remained weak in his presence. Nevertheless, I summoned the strength to break off contact with him. It was a necessary decision that had to be made.

With hindsight, I realize that I could have spared myself much heartache and confusion if I had listened to my intuition regarding this charming stranger's true nature. Moving forward, I have learned to be more vigilant in guarding my heart.

Sincerely,
Intuitively Connected

It's important to bear in mind that each person has a unique viewpoint. Be open to seeing the situation from the other person's perspective. Consider the mental, emotional, and spiritual resources available to them, or perhaps the lack thereof. Take accountability for your actions and contributions to the situation at hand. Evaluate whether your emotional reaction was proportionate to the severity of the situation. Were you able to forgive and move on, or did you find it difficult to do so? Above all, it's critical to adhere to the rules of engagement.

BREAK TO FIND YOUR WORTH

FIND YOUR WORTH TO REACH SELF-
ACTUALIZATION

REACH SELF-ACTUALIZATION TO
DISCOVER YOUR PURPOSE

DISCOVER YOUR PURPOSE TO ENTER
THE GATWAY TOWARDS

Ascension

love

A MOMENT FOR FREE THOUGHT

WHAT DO YOU EXPECT TO GET OUT OF THIS?

Shadow work is SELF work. Here is where you are completely transparent with yourself. This time isn't for anyone else. This is the time to set the tone for your healing. Get deep, very deep, and embrace any emotions that arise. Draw courage from within to face the inner shadow. Assess your feelings today and circle them on the feeling scale. Next, brainstorm self-care ideas you can complete while on this journey. On the next page, journal your thoughts and feelings. Reflect on your actions and ways you can improve them.

FEELING SCALE:

SELF-CARE IDEAS:

- _____
- _____
- _____
- _____
- _____
- _____
- _____
- _____

love →

DAY 1

DATE:

TOPIC

_____

FEELING SCALE

SELF-CARE PLAN

☐ _____

☐ _____

☐ _____

☐ _____

Remember your topic can be a situation from a previous day that you are still
working through or a new topic. Remember to address the what, who, when, and
where. How did it affect you? How have you grown from it? What did you learn?
What is your new strength?

TOPIC

_____

FEELING SCALE

SELF-CARE PLAN

☐ _____

☐ _____

☐ _____

☐ _____

Remember your topic can be a situation from a previous day that you are still working through or a new topic. Remember to address the what, who, when, and where. How did it affect you? How have you grown from it? What did you learn? What is your new strength?

TOPIC

_____

FEELING SCALE

SELF-CARE PLAN

☐ _____

☐ _____

☐ _____

☐ _____

Remember your topic can be a situation from a previous day that you are still working through or a new topic. Remember to address the what, who, when, and where. How did it affect you? How have you grown from it? What did you learn? What is your new strength?

Heartbreak is not solely an emotional ordeal; it can also take a physical and mental toll. It's intangible, and there is no pharmaceutical cure. The only way to deal with it is to allow time to pass and gradually fade the memory of it from your consciousness. Heartbreak often begins early in life, and it's not always related to romantic relationships. More often than not, it stems from a trusted individual who let us down in childhood. Unfortunately, many of us grow up burdened by the pain of our past and seek ways to heal. Sometimes, this may lead us to indulge in fleeting relationships that offer temporary relief from the previous hurt.

It's essential to recognize that every heartbreak is a reminder to cleanse ourselves of the pain and hurt of the past. It's vital to wash our own feet, to unburden ourselves from the baggage that we've been carrying around. It's time to let go and move forward, make yourself a priority, and a be servant of self care and love.

THE KEY TO GETTING OTHERS TO
VALUE YOU IS TO UNDERSTAND YOUR
OWN

Value

TOPIC

_____

FEELING SCALE

SELF-CARE PLAN

☐ _____

☐ _____

☐ _____

☐ _____

Remember your topic can be a situation from a previous day that you are still working through or a new topic. Remember to address the what, who, when, and where. How did it affect you? How have you grown from it? What did you learn? What is your new strength?

TOPIC

_____

FEELING SCALE

SELF-CARE PLAN

☐ _____

☐ _____

☐ _____

☐ _____

Remember your topic can be a situation from a previous day that you are still working through or a new topic. Remember to address the what, who, when, and where. How did it affect you? How have you grown from it? What did you learn? What is your new strength?

love →

TOPIC

_____

FEELING SCALE

SELF-CARE PLAN

☐ _____

☐ _____

☐ _____

☐ _____

Remember your topic can be a situation from a previous day that you are still working through or a new topic. Remember to address the what, who, when, and where. How did it affect you? How have you grown from it? What did you learn? What is your new strength?

TOPIC

_____

FEELING SCALE

SELF-CARE PLAN

☐ _____

☐ _____

☐ _____

☐ _____

Remember your topic can be a situation from a previous day that you are still working through or a new topic. Remember to address the what, who, when, and where. How did it affect you? How have you grown from it? What did you learn? What is your new strength?

Protection
Week 2

Once you have successfully cleansed from your past emotional wounds and released any negative thoughts and emotions associated with them, you may enter into the protection-building phase. It's important to note that protection doesn't equate to building a wall or isolating yourself; you are also isolating from positive experiences and people if you do that. You don't want to harden your heart or cut yourself off from all the good things that life has to offer.

During this period, you will be focusing on developing both mental and spiritual protection. This type of protection will help you develop discernment and provide a shield against negative spiritual attacks from external sources.

The process of building mental and spiritual protection is a crucial step in creating a secure and healthy life. It enables you to let go of past negativity and embrace a positive future while creating a safe space for growth and personal advancement. By opening yourself up to the guidance and protection of your ancestors, the creator, and your spirit guides, you are creating a shield that will help you navigate life's challenges with greater ease and grace. This type of protection will enable you to recognize negative influences and make wise choices that support your overall well-being. So, take the time to purify yourself of old wounds and negative emotions, and embrace the protection-building phase as an opportunity to manifest a bright and beautiful future for yourself.

NAVIGATING LIFE OFTEN REQUIRES
SUPPRESSING EMOTIONS WHILE
FEELING A DEEP INNER CALLING TO
CONFRONT PAINFUL TRUTHS.
SPIRITUALITY INVOLVES THE HUMAN
SPIRIT OR SOUL, RATHER THAN JUST
THE MATERIAL OR PHYSICAL ASPECTS
OF LIFE.

Spiritual Psychology

TOPIC

_____

FEELING SCALE

SELF-CARE PLAN

- [ ] _____
- [ ] _____
- [ ] _____
- [ ] _____

Remember your topic can be a situation from a previous day that you are still working through or a new topic. Remember to address the what, who, when, and where. How did it affect you? How have you grown from it? What did you learn? What is your new strength?

TOPIC

_____

FEELING SCALE

SELF-CARE PLAN

☐ _____

☐ _____

☐ _____

☐ _____

Remember your topic can be a situation from a previous day that you are still working through or a new topic. Remember to address the what, who, when, and where. How did it affect you? How have you grown from it? What did you learn? What is your new strength?

love →

TOPIC

_____

FEELING SCALE

SELF-CARE PLAN

☐ _____

☐ _____

☐ _____

☐ _____

Remember your topic can be a situation from a previous day that you are still
working through or a new topic. Remember to address the what, who, when, and
where. How did it affect you? How have you grown from it? What did you learn?
What is your new strength?

TOPIC

_____

FEELING SCALE

SELF-CARE PLAN

☐ _____

☐ _____

☐ _____

☐ _____

Remember your topic can be a situation from a previous day that you are still
working through or a new topic. Remember to address the what, who, when, and
where. How did it affect you? How have you grown from it? What did you learn?
What is your new strength?

Love is an incredibly potent force when it is genuine. Authentic love is not something that materializes overnight; rather, it requires patience and effort to establish a strong foundation that leads to genuine affection.

Simultaneously, learning to love oneself is a process that necessitates both introspection and self-care. To begin, it's essential to determine how one desires to be loved and then love oneself accordingly. Finally, it's crucial to communicate to the world how one wishes to be loved and cared for.

Regrettably, we often fixate on negative thoughts, allowing them to dominate our minds and affect our sense of self-worth. It's vital to reframe our mindset and focus on the positive aspects of oneself, reminding ourselves of our inherent goodness and worth.

IN A WORLD THAT FIXATES ON
ATTAINING PERFECTION, IT'S
ESSENTIAL TO COMPREHEND THAT THE
JOURNEY OF LIFE IS ONE THAT IS
INHERENTLY IMPERFECT, AND THAT IS
WHAT MAKES IT BEAUTIFUL. AS
INDIVIDUALS, WE ARE ALL UNIQUELY
FLAWED, AND IT'S THROUGH THESE
IMPERFECTIONS THAT WE CAN LEARN
AND GROW. RATHER THAN ASPIRING
FOR PERFECTION, WE SHOULD FOCUS
ON FINDING OUR TRUEST SELVES.

Imperfection

TOPIC

_____

FEELING SCALE

SELF-CARE PLAN

▢ _____

▢ _____

▢ _____

▢ _____

Remember your topic can be a situation from a previous day that you are still working through or a new topic. Remember to address the what, who, when, and where. How did it affect you? How have you grown from it? What did you learn? What is your new strength?

TOPIC

_____

FEELING SCALE

SELF-CARE PLAN

☐ _____

☐ _____

☐ _____

☐ _____

Remember your topic can be a situation from a previous day that you are still working through or a new topic. Remember to address the what, who, when, and where. How did it affect you? How have you grown from it? What did you learn? What is your new strength?

TOPIC

_____

FEELING SCALE

SELF-CARE PLAN

☐ _____

☐ _____

☐ _____

☐ _____

Remember your topic can be a situation from a previous day that you are still working through or a new topic. Remember to address the what, who, when, and where. How did it affect you? How have you grown from it? What did you learn? What is your new strength?

Love

Week 3

It's imperative to release any emotional baggage and establish healthy boundaries to protect yourself. At this point, it's vital to prioritize self-love, the most profound form of love. Surprisingly, we spend the most time with ourselves throughout our lives, making it crucial to recognize that solitude does not equate to loneliness. Instead, the journey of life is shared with our conscious mind and higher self. However, we often fail to connect with our shadow self, leading to a lack of self-love, exhaustion, and emotional drainage. Learning to nourish, heal, and embrace the shadow self is vital in developing infinite self-love. Embracing and accepting ourselves, acknowledging our strengths and weaknesses, and treating ourselves with kindness, compassion, and self-care is the beautiful journey towards self-discovery and self-acceptance. This journey requires continuous effort and patience, including setting boundaries to protect our energy, prioritizing self-care, and making choices that respect our well-being.

Once we learn to care for our inner selves, we'll feel grounded, centered, and fulfilled, radiating positivity and abundance outwards.

Loving ourselves is not selfish, but rather a selfless act that positively impacts our lives and those around us. Therefore, it's essential to nourish our souls, embrace our true selves, and pour love into ourselves every day.

INFUSE YOUR WORLD WITH LOVE

And live there

TOPIC

_____

FEELING SCALE

SELF-CARE PLAN

☐ _____

☐ _____

☐ _____

☐ _____

Remember your topic can be a situation from a previous day that you are still working through or a new topic. Remember to address the what, who, when, and where. How did it affect you? How have you grown from it? What did you learn? What is your new strength?

TOPIC

_____

FEELING SCALE

SELF-CARE PLAN

☐ _____

☐ _____

☐ _____

☐ _____

Remember your topic can be a situation from a previous day that you are still working through or a new topic. Remember to address the what, who, when, and where. How did it affect you? How have you grown from it? What did you learn? What is your new strength?

TOPIC

_____

FEELING SCALE

SELF-CARE PLAN

☐ _____

☐ _____

☐ _____

☐ _____

Remember your topic can be a situation from a previous day that you are still working through or a new topic. Remember to address the what, who, when, and where. How did it affect you? How have you grown from it? What did you learn? What is your new strength?

What type of character do you possess as a woman? Are you a kind, loving, patient, positive woman? What energy radiates from you? Is it a energy of peace? Is it welcoming? Is it home? Have you reflected on the current status of your previous partners? Are they married or single? Moreover, have you assessed your self–esteem, self–realization, and consciousness while involved with them? Can you confidently admit that you were a woman of high caliber – someone who had their education, career, debts, emotions, and mental state, all in check? As women, we ought to recognize our strengths and our weaknesses. Failure to do so may lead to unsuccessful relationships. Hence, take some time to reflect and assess what you bring to the table. Be what you expect from your partner.

I Love Me Jar

AS YOU GO THROUGH THIS PROCESS,
CONSIDER TAKING A JAR AND JOTTING
DOWN BRIEF NOTES OF POSITIVITY
AND ACCOMPLISHMENTS. YOU CAN
ALSO INCLUDE REMINDERS OF HOW
PROUD YOU ARE OF YOURSELF.
ADDITIONALLY, CONSIDER ASKING
LOVED ONES TO CONTRIBUTE NOTES
TO THE JAR AS WELL. THIS JAR
SERVES AS A SOURCE OF MOTIVATION
AND ENCOURAGEMENT DURING
CHALLENGING TIMES, HELPING TO
UPLIFT YOUR SPIRITS.

TOPIC

_____

FEELING SCALE

SELF-CARE PLAN

☐ _____

☐ _____

☐ _____

☐ _____

Remember your topic can be a situation from a previous day that you are still working through or a new topic. Remember to address the what, who, when, and where. How did it affect you? How have you grown from it? What did you learn? What is your new strength?

Letter from The Wise

Self-love did not come naturally. It took many years of failing to realize that all the love I needed started from within. My journey through self-neglect started when I was fifteen years old. I was looking for someone to love me and of course, my first boyfriend filled that void, but only verbally.

I had never been the popular girl in school and just the fact that I had a boyfriend was a big deal to me. Of course, I gave him my virginity in the bathroom of his Aunt's house. A couple of months later we were no longer boyfriend and girlfriend.
This became a trend. Meet a guy, fall for him, have sexual intercourse, and then break up within a year. I would leave these relationships feeling just as empty as I did when I entered them.

One day I had an epiphany, it wasn't the guys that I had chosen to date that were the "bad guys." I had let myself down. I chose men who did not have my best interest at heart, and they were visibly all about themselves.

It was then that I started to be selective about who I allowed in my life and my body. Doing this left me feeling free and in control. Feeling more in control of my life allowed me to see my worth and knowing my worth fostered self-love.

I'm sharing this with the hope that you will know that giving your heart and body to just anyone leaves an emptiness that will only be filled by YOU. Time to be your healer.

Sincerely,
Wise

Sacred Gateway

IT'S ESSENTIAL TO RECOGNIZE THAT
ESTABLISHING KARMIC BONDS AND
SPIRITUAL ATTACHMENTS CAN BE
POTENTIALLY HAZARDOUS. IN THIS
ERA, EACH DECISION WE MAKE
CARRIES SIGNIFICANT WEIGHT AND
CAN LEAD TO CONSEQUENCES. IT'S
CRUCIAL TO EXERCISE CAUTION WHEN
FORMING PHYSICAL CONNECTIONS AS
THEY OFTEN IMPRINT INTO THE SOUL.
PROTECT YOUR WOMB AS IT IS THE
DOORWAY TO THE SPIRITUAL REALM.

TOPIC

_____

FEELING SCALE

SELF-CARE PLAN

☐ _____

☐ _____

☐ _____

☐ _____

Remember your topic can be a situation from a previous day that you are still working through or a new topic. Remember to address the what, who, when, and where. How did it affect you? How have you grown from it? What did you learn? What is your new strength?

DATE:

TOPIC

_____

FEELING SCALE

SELF-CARE PLAN

☐ _____

☐ _____

☐ _____

☐ _____

Remember your topic can be a situation from a previous day that you are still
working through or a new topic. Remember to address the what, who, when, and
where. How did it affect you? How have you grown from it? What did you learn?
What is your new strength?

TOPIC

_____

FEELING SCALE

SELF-CARE PLAN

☐ _____
☐ _____
☐ _____
☐ _____

Remember your topic can be a situation from a previous day that you are still working through or a new topic. Remember to address the what, who, when, and where. How did it affect you? How have you grown from it? What did you learn? What is your new strength?

Afirm Your Dreams
Week 4

Now that you have established a solid foundation, you are ready to set your goals and pursue your aspirations. You should recognize your inherent strength, worth, and power. Dream big and bring those dreams to life through manifestation. There are various ways to manifest, including creating a vision board, engaging in spiritual practices and ritual work, or making a list and speaking your desires aloud. It's important to note that manifestation requires effort and action. Make decisions that align with your goals and take steps towards them daily, no matter how small.

To remain focused and motivated, surround yourself with positivity and individuals who support your dreams. Stay committed to your goals and celebrate every achievement, no matter how small. Don't let set backs discourage you; remember that manifestation is a process that may take time. Trust the timing of the universe and remain open to new opportunities and possibilities. With dedication, patience, and a positive mindset, you can bring the life of your dreams to fruition.

TRUSTING YOUR INTUITION CAN LEAD TO
DISCOVERING YOUR PURPOSE. GUIDES AND
TEACHERS CAN HELP INDIVIDUALS
UNDERSTAND THEIR INTUITION AND
CONNECT WITH A HIGHER POWER THAT
COMMUNICATES THROUGH DREAMS,
NUMBERS, SMALL VOICES, AND DÉJÀ VU.
INTUITION IS THE VOICE OF THE NON-
PHYSICAL PART OF ONESELF, COMMONLY
REFERRED TO AS THE GUT FEELING.

Purpose & Intuition

TOPIC

_____

FEELING SCALE

SELF-CARE PLAN

☐ _____

☐ _____

☐ _____

☐ _____

Remember your topic can be a situation from a previous day that you are still working through or a new topic. Remember to address the what, who, when, and where. How did it affect you? How have you grown from it? What did you learn? What is your new strength?

TOPIC

_____

FEELING SCALE

SELF-CARE PLAN

☐ _____

☐ _____

☐ _____

☐ _____

Remember your topic can be a situation from a previous day that you are still working through or a new topic. Remember to address the what, who, when, and where. How did it affect you? How have you grown from it? What did you learn? What is your new strength?

TOPIC

_____

FEELING SCALE

SELF-CARE PLAN

☐ _____

☐ _____

☐ _____

☐ _____

Remember your topic can be a situation from a previous day that you are still working through or a new topic. Remember to address the what, who, when, and where. How did it affect you? How have you grown from it? What did you learn? What is your new strength?

love →

TOPIC

DATE: _____

_____

FEELING SCALE

SELF-CARE PLAN

☐ _____

☐ _____

☐ _____

☐ _____

Remember your topic can be a situation from a previous day that you are still
working through or a new topic. Remember to address the what, who, when, and
where. How did it affect you? How have you grown from it? What did you learn?
What is your new strength?

The notion of forsaking all others often arises in discussions about marriage vows. However, have you ever pondered the idea of dedicating yourself to a committed relationship with yourself? In this relationship, you would prioritize self-love and self-protection just as much as you would for a partner or family member.

Perhaps the individuals you have prioritized in the past do not reciprocate your care or have your best interest at heart. Instead of dwelling on their actions, consider focusing on what you can do for yourself. Without self-worth and self-love, you may struggle to stand up against those who mean you harm and continually invite individuals who use and exploit you. There's no better time than now to start prioritizing yourself and forsaking all others. It's time to shake off the negative influences and embrace self-love and self-worth.

The Tree

HAS VERY FEW ROOTS, SEVERAL BRANCHES, AND A TON OF LEAVES. EACH SERVE THEIR OWN PURPOSE. LET'S START WITH THE PRETTY LEAVES. THEY COME WHEN THE WEATHER IS NICE AND SWAY IN THE WIND. WHEN THE WEATHER GETS COLD, THEY FALL OFF, LEAVING THE TREE BARE AND NOT AS BEAUTIFUL AS IT USED TO BE. ALL YOU SEE IS THE BRANCHES. NOW THE BRANCHES, THEY HOLD ON FOR YEARS, MAYBE A DECADE OR TWO, BUT EVENTUALLY THOSE FALL OFF AS WELL. NEITHER THE LEAVES NOR THE BRANCHES GIVE THE TREE LIFE. YOU KNOW WHAT DOES THOUGH? THE ROOTS. THE ROOTS OF A TREE ARE FEW AND HIDDEN, BUT THEY LAST A LIFETIME. THEY REMAIN TO NURTURE AND CONSTANTLY GIVE THE TREE LIFE EVEN IN THE WORSE SEASON. YOU ARE THE TREE. LEARN TO IDENTIFY YOUR LEAVES, BRANCHES, AND ROOTS.

TOPIC

_____

FEELING SCALE

SELF-CARE PLAN

- ☐ _____
- ☐ _____
- ☐ _____
- ☐ _____

Remember your topic can be a situation from a previous day that you are still working through or a new topic. Remember to address the what, who, when, and where. How did it affect you? How have you grown from it? What did you learn? What is your new strength?

TOPIC

_____

FEELING SCALE

SELF-CARE PLAN

☐ _____

☐ _____

☐ _____

☐ _____

Remember your topic can be a situation from a previous day that you are still
working through or a new topic. Remember to address the what, who, when, and
where. How did it affect you? How have you grown from it? What did you learn?
What is your new strength?

TOPIC

_____

FEELING SCALE

SELF-CARE PLAN

☐ _____

☐ _____

☐ _____

☐ _____

Remember your topic can be a situation from a previous day that you are still
working through or a new topic. Remember to address the what, who, when, and
where. How did it affect you? How have you grown from it? What did you learn?
What is your new strength?

love →

DATE: ▢

TOPIC

_____

FEELING SCALE

SELF-CARE PLAN

☐ _____

☐ _____

☐ _____

☐ _____

Remember your topic can be a situation from a previous day that you are still working through or a new topic. Remember to address the what, who, when, and where. How did it affect you? How have you grown from it? What did you learn? What is your new strength?

TOPIC

_____

FEELING SCALE

SELF-CARE PLAN

☐ _____

☐ _____

☐ _____

☐ _____

Remember your topic can be a situation from a previous day that you are still
working through or a new topic. Remember to address the what, who, when, and
where. How did it affect you? How have you grown from it? What did you learn?
What is your new strength?

Reflection

Discover the silver lining in your present circumstance. Although it might be difficult to accept, recognize that you are precisely where you're supposed to be at this moment. If you've reached this point in your journey, you've undoubtedly grown stronger, better, and more grounded than you were thirty days ago. You can always restart your thirty-day journey to continue your spiritual progress and interact with your shadow self. This partnership is sacred and is designed to help guide you through all of your spiritual endeavors. Above all, cultivating a relationship with your inner self is paramount.

Self Exposure

IT'S A PROFOUND REALIZATION WHEN WE ACKNOWLEDGE THAT HEALING TRANSCENDS THE BOUNDARIES OF OUR PHYSICAL EXISTENCE. IT'S A PROCESS THAT AFFECTS THE SOUL AT A DEEPER LEVEL. TO COMPREHEND THIS, IT'S ESSENTIAL TO VIEW OURSELVES AS STUDENTS, UNDERGOING A SESSION OF SOUL HEALING. BY ASKING OURSELVES, "WHO AM I?" WE EMBARK ON A JOURNEY OF SELF-DISCOVERY THAT NEVER TRULY ENDS.

Mental Health Resources

Blackmentalwellness.com

Melaninandmentalhealth.com

Telemynd.com

Inclusivetherapists.com